Milly, Molly
What was that?

"We may look different but we feel the same."

It was spring. Farmer Hegarty's ewes were ready to have their lambs.

"I think Bunty will be first," he said.
"She must go into the barn for the night."
"Won't she be lonely?" asked Milly.

"Never," replied Farmer Hegarty. "A barn is the busiest place in the world at night."
"Can we keep Bunty company?" asked Molly.
"You can," replied Farmer Hegarty, "but don't count on getting any sleep."

Milly, Molly and Bunty tucked down in the hay for the night.

"Ricket ricket. Ricket ricket."
"What was that?"
"Only a cricket calling to his friends," said Bunty softly. "Now go off to sleep."

Flutter, flutter, flutter.
"What was that?"
"A swallow, settling in for the night," yawned Bunty. "Back to sleep you go."

Scurry, scurry.
"What was that?"
"Just a mouse going about her business," whispered Bunty. "Close your eyes."

"Reeoow."
"What was that?"
"The barn cat stretching,"
explained Bunty softly. "Now lie down."

Rattle rattle. Rattle rattle.

"What was that?"

"Only a rat stashing his walnuts," said Bunty quietly. "Turn over and go to sleep."

"Whooo, Whooo."

"What was that?"

"The night owl hooting his whereabouts," said Bunty sleepily. "Don't be afraid."

"Puk puk, puk puk."
"What was that?"
"A hen gathering in her chicks," yawned Bunty.
"Snuggle down and close your eyes."

Flap flap, flap.
"What was that?"
"Just a bat coming in from the night," whispered Bunty. "You are perfectly safe."

Snuffle, snuffle, snuffle.

"What was that?"

"Only a hedgehog searching for his dinner," explained Bunty softly. "Settle down again."

"Cock-a-doodle-doo." "What was that?"
"That was the rooster," said Bunty quietly. "Roll over and get some sleep before
the sun comes up."

At last the barn was quiet.
Milly and Molly were fast asleep but
Bunty had something else on her mind.

She stood up.

She sat down.

She stood up again.

She lay down. But she didn't make a noise.

When Farmer Hegarty
peeped into the barn at daybreak
he couldn't believe his eyes.

"Hello, hello."
"What was that?"
"That was Farmer Hegarty," said Bunty softly.
"It's time to get up."

"Baa, baa."
"Bunty, what was that?"

"A lamb each for keeping me company."